A World of Festivals

Life and Death

Jean Coppendale

Chrysalis Children's Books

First published in the UK in 2003 by
Chrysalis Children's Books
The Chrysalis Building, Bramley Road, London W10 6SP

ISBN 184138 8432

British Library Cataloguing in Publication Data for this book is available from the British Library.

A Belitha Book
Editorial Manager: Joyce Bentley
Assistant Editor: Clare Chambers

Produced by
Tall Tree Ltd
Editor: Jon Richards
Consultant: Stephanie Batley
Picture Researcher: Dan Brooks
Artwork: Piers Harper

Printed in China

10 9 8 7 6 5 4 3 2 1

PICTURE CREDITS
All reasonable efforts have been made to trace the relevant copyright holders of the images contained within this book. If we were unable to reach you, please contact Chrysalis Books.

B = bottom; C = centre; L = left; R = right; T = top.
Corbis – 7, 8, 18, 19, 21. **Eye Ubiquitous** – back cover, 1, 4, 5, 6, 10, 11, 12, 14, 15, 16, 22, 24, 25, 26, 27. **James Davies Worldwide Travel Library** – front cover C, 13.
Sonia Halliday Photographs – 20. **Spectrum Colour Library** – 17, 23.

Contents

Introduction

Many ceremonies are held at the start of a person's life, to welcome him or her, or at their death, to say goodbye.

This couple is preparing their baby for a **christening**.

Societies all around the world have ceremonies that welcome a new baby and help prepare him or her for a happy life.

This father and daughter are saying goodbye to a close relative who has died.

The death of a loved one may be a time of celebration as well as a time of sadness. Some cultures have festivals every year to remember the dead.

Naming a Child

There are lots of ceremonies where children are welcomed and named.

This christening is taking place on the Pacific island of Tonga.

Christening
Christian children are named in a christening or baptism. A priest or minister pours water over the baby's head to **bless** the child.

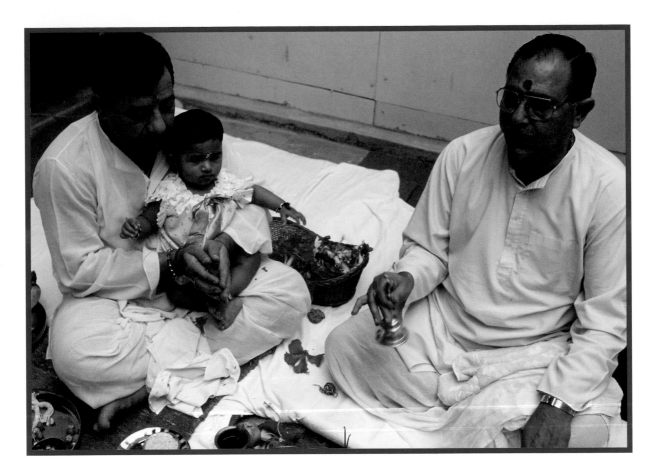

Before shaving a Hindu baby's head, the priest says special prayers and rings a **temple** bell.

Hindu naming

Hindus have several ceremonies to welcome and name a new child. At the end, the child's hair is shaved off to remove any bad luck.

FESTIVAL FACT

During the Hindu naming ceremonies, people eat a special food, called prasadami, made from nuts, sweets and fruit.

Giving a Name

In addition to naming the children, ceremonies are thought to protect them from evil.

Young Buddhist monks are often invited to preach at a naming ceremony.

Buddhist naming

In a Thai Buddhist naming ceremony, the baby is put into a special cradle which is then filled with gifts. Boys are given books and tools, and girls are given needles and threads.

A trick name is written on a plaque and given to the child. This plaque reads 'Dog Face' in Chinese.

Trick names

Some Chinese children are given a trick name. This is done to confuse evil spirits who might want to steal the child.

FESTIVAL FACT

Chinese people do not celebrate birthdays. Instead, all Chinese people are one year older on New Year's Day.

Dassehra

Dassehra is one of many festivals around the world that celebrate good winning over evil and people being saved from death.

People take part in a procession on the day of Dassehra and act out the story of Rama and Sita.

Gods and demons

During Dassehra, Hindus remember the story of the god Rama. He saved his wife Sita from a wicked demon called Ravana.

Inside the statue of Ravana are fireworks which explode as the statue burns.

Fireworks

On the last night of the festival, a huge straw and cardboard statue of Ravana is set alight.

FESTIVAL DIARY

Dassehra
Hindu
September or October

Day of the Dead

The Day of the Dead is celebrated in Latin America. People remember and celebrate the lives of loved ones who have died.

Some of the **offerings** to the dead are small skulls made from sugar and water.

Graves and offerings

During this Catholic festival, people visit the graves of friends and family and leave offerings to the dead.

Many people make colourful masks to wear.

Colourful costumes
Some people also dress up in bright, colourful costumes, while others dress up as skeletons.

FESTIVAL DIARY

Day of the Dead
Latin America
1 November

O-Bon

O-Bon is a Japanese Buddhist festival where people place food offerings to the dead on their family's **altars**.

These Japanese women are performing a dance called Bon Odori.

Lighting lanterns

People light lanterns, called chouchin, and perform traditional folk dances.

These huge drums are called taiko.
They are played to accompany the Bon
Odori dancers.

Music and dancing
Bon Odori dancers are
usually accompanied
by traditional Japanese
musical instruments.

**FESTIVAL
DIARY**

O-Bon
Japan
July or August

Hungry Ghosts

Many people believe that ghosts come back to haunt the living and need gifts to keep them happy.

People give food and burn paper gifts to please the ghosts during Hsia Yuan.

Hsia Yuan

Hsia Yuan is also known as the Festival of Hungry Ghosts. People try to keep ghosts happy and stop them from causing trouble.

People carve dragons and wear masks with scary faces to frighten off the ghosts.

Magic sword

During one ceremony for Hsia Yuan, priests wave a magic sword to scare the ghosts away.

FESTIVAL DIARY

Hsia Yuan
China
August

Ghosts and Spirits

Some ceremonies honour the dead and help them to find peace after their death.

After the Procession of the Cows, everyone dresses up to celebrate.

Gai Jatra

This festival is also known as the Procession of the Cows. It is thought that cows help a dead person on his or her journey to heaven.

Vu Lan is also celebrated in temples where prayers are said for dead people.

Vu Lan

During Vu Lan, or Wandering Souls Day, families visit the graves of loved ones to honour the dead.

FESTIVAL DIARY

Gai Jatra
Nepal and Tibet
August or September

Vu Lan
Vietnam
August

Burying the Dead

Funerals are times of great ceremony when special prayers are said for the dead person.

In some Jewish funerals the body is wrapped in a long cloth, called a shroud.

Jewish funeral

Flowers are not allowed at a Jewish funeral. During the service, the closest male relative reads a prayer called the kaddish.

In a Muslim funeral, the body is buried facing towards the holy Muslim city of Mecca.

Muslim funeral

A Muslim funeral often takes place the day after the person has died. The coffin is taken to a **mosque**, where the **Imam** says a special funeral prayer.

FESTIVAL FACT

Muslim families spend three months in **mourning** after the death of a relative.

Christian Funeral

A Christian funeral usually takes place four or five days after a person has died.

The coffin is carried by close friends and family members.

Coffins
The body is placed in a coffin. It is either buried in a **cemetery** or burnt at a crematorium and the ashes are buried or scattered.

Often flowers and **wreaths** are carried on the coffin and placed on the grave.

Headstones

Many Christian graves are marked by a **headstone**. The person's name and the years they lived are usually written on it.

FESTIVAL FACT

A celebration of the person's life is usually held after a funeral. This party is called a wake.

Chinese Funeral

During a Chinese funeral, there are ceremonies to help the soul of the dead person on the journey to heaven.

Mourners at a Chinese funeral wear white.

Loud noises
Musicians playing drums and cymbals follow the coffin to the cemetery, and fireworks are set off to scare away evil spirits.

A paper car is burnt as an offering at a Chinese funeral.

Offerings

At the grave, offerings are burnt for the dead person to use in the afterlife. These include fake money, paper houses and paper cars.

FESTIVAL FACT

A Chinese coffin is buried for ten years, then the bones are dug up and put into a special pot.

Cremation

Some religions and cultures always cremate, or burn, the bodies of dead people.

A Hindu funeral **pyre** is lit by the eldest son of the dead person.

Hindu funeral

In a Hindu funeral, the body is placed on a large bonfire of wood, called a pyre.

These musicians are wearing colourful costumes at a Buddhist funeral.

Buddhist funeral

Buddhist funerals are happy occasions. This is because Buddhists believe that people are reborn after they die. Each time this happens, they are a step closer to God.

FESTIVAL FACT

After the Buddhist funeral service, the body is cremated and the ashes are buried or kept in a temple.

Try This!

Ask an adult to help you with these activities.

Make a Chinese name disc

You will need:
- thin red card
- dinner plate
- pencil

- scissors
- gold or black paint
- thin string

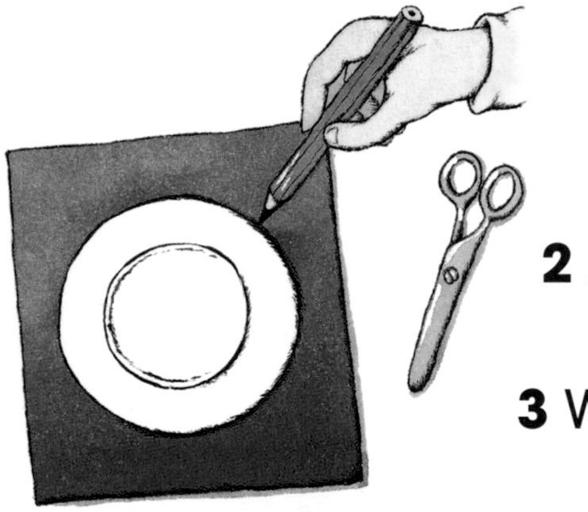

1 Put the dinner plate face down on the card. Carefully draw around it in pencil.

2 Ask an adult to cut out the circle.

3 Write the name you choose in pencil on the disc. Copy the design shown here which means 'Beautiful Flower', or use 'Dog Face' from page eight.

4 Then, using the gold or black paint, trace over the name.

5 Using the scissors, make small holes on either side of the disc. Thread the string through the holes, making sure that the string fits comfortably over your head, and tie small knots to secure it.

Make a Day of the Dead skeleton puppet

You will need:
- picture of a skeleton to copy
- thin black cardboard
- scissors
- white paint
- hole punch
- five paper fasteners
- ice-lolly stick
- string

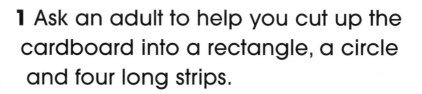

1 Ask an adult to help you cut up the cardboard into a rectangle, a circle and four long strips.

2 Paint the bones of a skeleton onto the pieces of cardboard.

3 Punch a hole at the joints and join the pieces with paper fasteners.

4 Thread some string through the top of the skull and through each hand and tie the ends in a knot.

5 Tie the other ends to the lolly stick. Your skeleton is now ready to dance!

How to Say...

Bon Odori
say *bon o-door-ee*

Chouchin
say *choo-chin*

Christening
say *chriss-en-ing*

Cremation
say *cree-may-shun*

Dassehra
say *das-say-ra*

Gai Jatra
say *gai jat-ra*

Hsia Yuan
say *see-ah yoo-an*

Kaddish
say *ka-dish*

O-Bon
say *oh bon*

Prasadami
say *pra-sa-da-mee*

Pyre
say *pie-er*

Ravana
say *ra-va-na*

Taiko
say *tie-ko*

Vu Lan
say *voo lan*

Glossary

Altar
A special area in a temple, church, synagogue, mosque or home where religious ceremonies are performed.

Bless
To ask a god to protect a child or an object.

Cemetery
A special area of ground, separate from a church or temple, where the bodies of dead people are taken and buried.

Christening
The Christian ceremony during which a baby is blessed, named and welcomed into the church.

Cremation
A service during which the body of a dead person is burned. The ashes are then buried or scattered over a special place.

Headstone
A headstone is a carved stone that marks a grave.

Imam
A Muslim religious leader.

Latin America
Areas of America where the people speak Spanish or Portuguese, such as South America and Central America.

Mosque
A Muslim place of worship.

Mourning
This is when friends feel sad about the death of a person. People wear special clothes to show that they are in mourning.

Offerings
Gifts made to help the spirits of the dead in the afterlife, or to keep ghosts and gods happy.

Pyre
A pile of wood on which dead people are burned, or cremated.

Temple
A building that is used for prayer.

Wreath
A circle of flowers that is placed on a grave.

Index